WAR IN YUGOSLAVIA

The Breakup of a Nation

Edward R. Ricciuti

Evans

Evans Brothers Limited

First published in the United States by The Millbrook Press, Brookfield, Connecticut

Published in Great Britain in 1993 by Evans Brothers Limited
2A Portman Mansions
Chiltern Street
London W1M 1LE

First published in Great Britain in 1993
Reprinted 1995.

Printed in Spain by GRAFO, S.A. - Bilbao

ISBN 0 237 51366 8

Contents

4

Chapter 1

The Balkan Tinderbox

As the home of more than 140,000 schoolchildren and students, Sarajevo used to be called "city of the young". In the spring of 1992 that all changed, and Sarajevo quickly became the "city of death". Ignited by internal hatreds, the historic capital of the former Yugoslavian republic of Bosnia-Herzegovina (or simply "Bosnia") exploded into a battleground.

Mortar and artillery shells rained upon the beautiful old buildings of Sarajevo. Small-arms fire from scattered snipers crackled day and night. Thousands of people— mostly civilians—were killed and wounded. Sarajevo had become another victim of the internal war that, since the summer of 1991, had violently ripped apart the nation that used to be Yugoslavia.

The conflict in Yugoslavia has been one of the most savage wars in recent history. By midsummer 1992, at least 10,000 people had perished. Some estimates put the dead at more than 40,000. Thousands of other people had been wounded. And more than two million others became refugees, the most in Europe since World War II. Fearful atrocities were committed by all sides. Innocent people were tortured and murdered. Even children and the elderly became victims of brutal revenge killings.

During the summer of 1991, deep-seated ethnic hatreds erupted into a brutal and widespread war.

Opposite:
Civilians lie dead after a bomb in their car exploded on the streets of Sarajevo, the capital of Bosnia.

The fighting in Yugoslavia erupted between members of different ethnic and religious groups. They are not new enemies. Their animosity is rooted deep in the past.

Yugoslavia's bloody troubles have been called a civil war, but in many ways, that is not the most accurate description. As a country, Yugoslavia did not exist until after World War I. It was patched together out of various peoples and small countries. The peoples who suddenly became "Yugoslavs" had their own ethnic and religious identities. Many never thought of themselves as Yugoslavs. However, the majority of them shared a similar racial makeup.

Because the former Yugoslavian republic was really a "patchwork" of peoples who were forced together, ethnic hatreds had brewed for many years. When they finally exploded, they exploded with great force and brutality. Once the Yugoslavian coalition began to fall apart, it became apparent to members of the international community that conflict was a real danger on many fronts in the region. Bloody violence in Bosnia, Croatia, and Slovenia was the main problem at hand but, as the violence escalated, world leaders became more concerned by the threat that the war could spread to other Balkan regions. The regions most in danger included the Serbian province of Kosovo, Albania, Bulgaria, the former Yugoslavian republic of Macedonia, and Greece. Albania, Greece, and Bulgaria—longtime enemies in their own right—had, between them, interests in Kosovo and Macedonia. By the autumn of 1992, all five regions seemed poised to enter the fray if they felt provoked.

Ethnic Divisions

The name *Yugoslavia* means "land of the South Slavs". The vast majority of people within its boundaries are Slavs, one of Europe's largest ethnic groups. But the Yugoslavs are divided into smaller factions that have historically been enemies, or have at least intensely disliked one another.

Modern Yugoslavia was put together by the great European powers after World War I. Following World War II, Yugoslavia was ruled by the Communist Marshal Tito (his real name was Josip Broz). Under Tito, a Communist Yugoslavian federation was created. It was made up of six republics: Serbia, Montenegro, Croatia, Slovenia, Bosnia-Herzegovina and Macedonia. Each had its own government and also took part in the federal government.

Each republic was dominated by a different group of Yugoslavs. Members of all groups, however, were scattered throughout the country. Many felt more loyalty to their own people than to the federation. Tito, a strong leader, held them together, but after he died in 1980, the nation slowly began to crumble. So did the Communist party. By the end of the 1980s, the power of the Communists in Yugoslavia had almost completely dissipated.

Beginning of the Breakup

By 1990, the Yugoslavian republics were headed on a collision course. On June 25, 1991, Slovenia and Croatia declared their independence. Macedonia and Bosnia followed.

All that remained of the Yugoslavian federation was Serbia—the most powerful of the republics—and tiny Montenegro. Yugoslavia still had a federal government, but its power was taken over by the government of Serbia.

The Serbian population is the largest in what used to be Yugoslavia. The Serbs number nine million of the former country's twenty-three million people. Most Serbs live in Serbia, but more than a tenth of Croatia's people are also Serbs. Almost one third of Bosnia's population is Serbian. Montenegrins, and many Macedonians, were originally of Serbian stock. Over centuries, however, these peoples formed their own distinct national identities. Of them all, the Serbs have the most established history of being a united country. Many Serbs want their own unique country to emerge again, whatever the cost to others.

Most Serbs belong to the Orthodox Church, which split from the Roman Catholic Church in the eleventh century. Croats are mostly Roman Catholics, with ties to Germany and Austria. Split along religious lines, these two nations are ancient foes of the Serbs. The majority of Bosnians are Slavic Muslims. They converted to Islam under the Muslim Turks, who ruled most of the Balkans until late in the nineteenth century.

Although there were tensions, many Yugoslavians of different ethnic groups lived side by side without trouble for many years. Often they were good neighbours. But deep-seated hatreds always bubbled close to the surface.

By the late 1980s and early 1990s, many Serbs in Croatia and Bosnia decided they no longer wanted to be citizens of their respective independent republics. They believed Serbs should be ruled only by other Serbs.

Fuelled by growing resentments, the Serbian nationalists rebelled against the governments of Croatia and Bosnia in 1991. Their aim was to carve out new Serbian territories that were within the newly independent states.

The Serbian government welcomed the allegiance of Serbs in the other republics. International observers and

ETHNIC MAJORITIES OF THE REPUBLICS

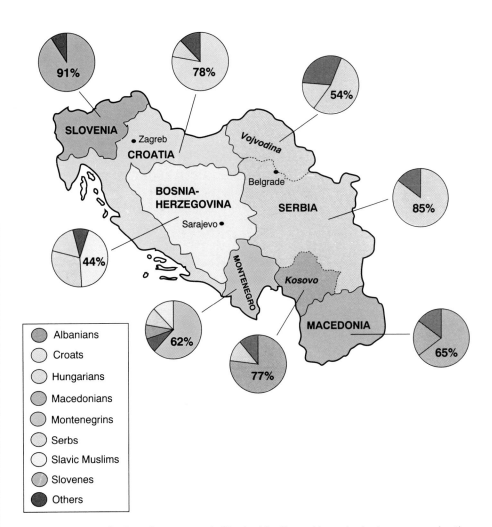

Besides the Serbs, Croats, and Slavic Muslims, Yugoslavia has several other peoples. The Montenegrins are closely tied by religion and blood with the Serbs. The Slovenes, centred in Slovenia, are mainly Roman Catholic. Macedonians are largely Orthodox and have strong ethnic ties to both Slavs and Greeks. There are two provinces in Serbia that are largely self-governing. The majority of people in the province of Kosovo are of Albanian blood and Muslim faith. Vojvodina has large numbers of Hungarians and Slovaks, mostly Roman Catholic. Other ethnic groups in Yugoslavia include Italians, Romanians and Bulgarians. There are many Germans in Croatia.

A Croatian soldier fires a bazooka from a roof in Sarajevo during a clash with Serbian forces in the summer of 1992.

analysts believed the Serbian government wanted to create a "Greater Serbia" that would include parts of Croatia and Bosnia, where many Serbs lived. The Serbian government aided—in many ways even helped to start—rebellions in Croatia and Bosnia that quickly erupted into war.

International Attempts for Peace

As happened at the start of World War I, other nations in the world took a stand when the Yugoslavian conflict of 1991 first erupted. This time, however, the other nations were not trying to fan the flames of war; they wanted to quench them. Most of the world's major powers blamed Serbia for provoking a needless battle. The European Community (EC) and the United States, together with the United Nations, worked feverishly to stop the war, but the task seemed almost impossible. The peacemakers were not only up against modern politics, but they faced a complex history of ancient fears and hatreds that stood squarely in the way of peace.

Not all Serbs were in favour of war over the issue of Serbian self-rule. A Serbian woman who worked at the Belgrade airport was one of those people. Her husband, she said, was a Croat. She had a son who was eligible for military service. "The war," she said, was "irrational." She added that she believed most people didn't want the war, and she blamed the political leaders on all sides. "The leaders are out of control," she said. "They fan the hate."

The leaders of whom she spoke were Serbian president Slobodan Milosevic and Croatian president Franjo Tudjman. Both men were strong-willed and stubborn dictators, and many observers held them responsible for starting the war.

Tudjman and Milosevic had much in common. Both were known as "tough guys". Both were prominent hard-line Communist officials under Marshal Tito. Tudjman was an army general who began to favour Croatian nationalism over communism in the 1970s. Just months before Croatia declared independence, he was elected president on a platform that promised sovereignty for Croatia. Some observers believed that Tudjman used the idea of independence simply as a way to gain power. Milosevic stayed with the Communist party until it folded, and some observers believed he remained a Communist at heart. His avowed affiliation was with the Socialist party, which was formerly the Communist party. Some observers also believed that he had pushed Serbian nationalism primarily as a way to stay in power.

Chapter 2

Roots of Hatred

The roots of the conflict in Yugoslavia go back more than 1,500 years, to the time soon after the fall of the Roman Empire. During the fifth century, tribes of Slavs moved south from the Carpathian Mountains of central Europe. Within a century, these tribes had permanently settled throughout much of the region that became Yugoslavia.

Foreign Influences

By the seventh and eighth centuries, various groups of Slavs had fallen under the influence of more powerful peoples who invaded from outside Yugoslavia. This domination by foreign forces would affect their future, right up to the present day.

During the late eighth century and early ninth century, the Slovenes became subjects of German counts, and the Croats were ruled by the Franks, a Germanic people who had earlier settled in France. German and Frankish missionaries converted both groups to the Western Rite of Roman Catholicism. Serbo-Croatian ties to Germanic, Roman Catholic culture still exist. The Slovenes, in fact, remained under German or Austrian sway until the end of World War II in 1945.

Religious
and ethnic
differences
combined with
a history of
oppression
created
enemies for
generations.

Opposite:
A victim of the war is buried in a cemetery in Bosnia.

The Serbs came under the rule of the Byzantine Greek Empire and followed the Eastern Rite of Catholicism. During the eleventh century, the Eastern Rite severed ties with the Roman Church and became the Orthodox faith. Thus began the religious differences that today separate the Serbs from the Croats and Slovenes.

Domination in the Middle Ages

The Middle Ages were violent in Yugoslavia. Montenegro, then called Zeta, led a successful Serb rebellion against the ruling Byzantines. Serbia soon became a powerful kingdom and provided a basis for the strong national identity that Serbs have today. Croatia, meanwhile, joined with Hungary. Bosnia was caught in the middle of the conflicts between Croatia and Serbia (as it was in the 1990s) and was ruled by Hungary and Croatia.

Toward the end of the fourteenth century, the Ottoman Turks invaded the Balkans, and by the fifteenth century, they ruled most of what became Yugoslavia. Somehow, the Montenegrins managed to keep the Turks out. The southern coast of Croatia was held by Venice, and a military frontier was established in northern Croatia by the Austrian Empire, chief opponent of the Turks.

Turkish power peaked at the start of the seventeenth century. Gradually, the Austrians and their allies, together with Slav rebels, chipped away at Turkish holdings. It was a long and bloody process that would go on for more than three hundred years. During that time, Croatia was given to Austria.

The Birth of Modern Yugoslavia

After Serbia gained its independence in 1878, it fought several wars, the first of which was against Bulgaria. In 1912, however, Serbia joined with Bulgaria, Montenegro, and Greece to drive the Turks out of their last Ottoman footholds in Yugoslavia. A year later, Serbia and Greece

Opposite:
A depiction of the Ottoman Turks in battle during the sixteenth century. The Turks invaded the Balkans in the late 1300s and dominated the region for more than five hundred years.

After World War I, King Alexander headed a new country called the Kingdom of Serbs, Croats, and Slovenes.

fought Bulgaria. The treaty that ended the war gave Macedonia to Serbia. The shifting alliances that occurred during this period were typical of the shaky governments in the Balkan states at the time.

Serbia fought the Austro-Hungarians, the Germans, and the Bulgarians during World War I. After the war, the map of Europe was completely redrawn. The prince of Serbia, Alexander, was made the head of a new country that was called the Kingdom of Serbs, Croats and Slovenes. It included most of modern Yugoslavia.

Alexander's infant kingdom was an uneasy one. Non-Serbs, especially Croats and Macedonians, resisted Serbian domination and, in 1929, an angry King Alexander proclaimed his dictatorship over a new country to be called the Kingdom of Yugoslavia. The king's actions only made things worse. Five years later, while in France, Alexander was assassinated. Scholars believe Croatian nationalists were responsible. Alexander's young son, Peter, assumed the throne, but since he was still a boy, Alexander's cousin, Prince Paul, was authorized to run the kingdom.

World War II

As World War II loomed in 1939, Yugoslavia was in turmoil. Hoping to calm growing Croatian unrest, the government gave Croatia a large measure of self-rule. But the situation inside Yugoslavia only worsened, and the Croats and Serbs were soon embroiled in conflict.

What happened in Yugoslavia during World War II cemented the foundation upon which the conflict of the 1990s was based. Yugoslavs had fought bravely and viciously against their occupiers—and one another—but the country, with its ethnic and religious mix of peoples, came apart at the seams when the war ended. Looking back at those postwar circumstances makes it easier to understand the complicated and tragic situation that eventually came to a head in the early 1990s.

The Balkan Battleground

War is no stranger to Yugoslavia, which lies partly on the Balkan Peninsula. Collectively, Yugoslavia, Greece, Albania, and other countries of the region are known as the "Balkans". For centuries, the Balkans have been a battleground upon which countries have fought one another as well as outsiders.

The Balkans have been called a "tinderbox" by many political analysts. Indeed, ever since an assassination in Sarajevo, on June 28, 1914, ignited World War I, the Balkans have been unstable politically.

On that infamous June day, a Bosnian student revolutionary named Gavrilo Princip shot and killed the Archduke Franz Ferdinand, who was heir to the throne of the powerful Austro-Hungarian Empire. (Austria and Hungary had joined forces in 1867.) Austria-Hungary controlled Bosnia and threatened Serbia.

The assassination was plotted by a Serbian nationalist group known as the "Black Hand." (This group had no connection to the Mafia, which was then also known as the "Black Hand".)

As punishment for the murder, Austria-Hungary threatened to take over Serbia. Austria-Hungary had been worried that the Serbs had become too powerful. The shooting gave Austria-Hungary a perfect excuse to humble and weaken the Serbian coalition that could have potentially gained real power.

As tensions increased, Germany sided with Austria-Hungary. Russia, the most powerful Slavic nation, supported Serbia. Before the end of the summer of 1914, Germany and Austria-Hungary were warring with Russia and its allies, France and Britain. The world had become engulfed by war.

Assassin Gavrilo Princip.

Archduke Franz Ferdinand and his wife minutes before their assassination.

By 1941, Yugoslavia was almost surrounded by German and Italian forces (the Axis). The government under Prince Paul signed a treaty with the two Axis powers, but the agreement was yet another bad idea that ignited prompt civil unrest.

Many Yugoslavs resented the treaty. Two days after it was signed, army officers took over the government and ousted Prince Paul. Alexander's son Peter was made king.

Less than two weeks after Peter's coronation, a horde of Axis enemies invaded Yugoslavia. With the Germans and Italians were Hungarians, Bulgarians and Albanians. The

Townspeople from the Croatian hamlet of Knin pose in their traditional clothing shortly before the outbreak of World War II.

war ended in a couple of weeks, leaving Peter and his Yugoslavian government helpless. Peter signed an armistice with the Axis powers and left for England.

The terms of the armistice carved up Yugoslavia into little bits, each bit meant to satisfy a different interest. Germany and Italy shared Slovenia. Italy grabbed the Adriatic coast of Croatia and also established a puppet government in Montenegro. Albania was given Kosovo. Hungary was given land near its border. Bulgaria occupied Macedonia. And in Belgrade, the capital of Serbia and Yugoslavia, the Germans set up a puppet state.

On April 10, 1941, while Yugoslavia was carved up, the government of Croatia proclaimed itself an independent state. It had been sympathetic to the Germans and Italians during the war. For its allegiance, Croatia was given Bosnia. Later, when Italy surrendered, Croatia was also given the Adriatic coast, which it retains to the present day.

With Axis backing, the Croatian government, called Ustasha, took action against Serbs and Jews. It tried to force Orthodox Serbs in the lands it controlled to convert to Roman Catholicism and pledge allegiance to Croatian leadership. Serbs who resisted were killed, as were

Yugoslavian Jews. The Croatian government assisted the Nazi Germans in their campaign of extermination against the Jews. All told, more than 1.5 million Serbs and Jews were killed by the Croatian government. Some Croats served in the German army, including the dreaded SS. The Serbs have not forgotten what happened in World War II. Many of them still have great hatred and very real fear of Croats. (Some Muslims also aided the Nazis.)

Early in the recent civil war, a Serbian tour guide expressed the long-standing fear of Croats to an inquiring foreign reporter. At first, however, the Serb voiced his dissatisfaction over the war. "It is a stupid war," he said. "It will ruin the country. Already it has destroyed tourism and the money it brings."

Then he paused for a moment.

"But you have to remember," he continued, "what happened in World War II. They [the Croats] killed many Serbs. Sometimes they lined up the Serbs in concentration camps and slit their throats."

The Yugoslavian Resistance

The Yugoslavs were a strong and determined group of people. The Germans and Italians found that out when they marched into Yugoslavia during World War II.

Within a few months of the Axis invasion, Yugoslav resistance units formed. One group, the Chetniks, was organized by a Yugoslav army general named Draza Mihailovic. The group's aim was to restore Peter to the throne and with him, Serbian dominance in Yugoslavia.

Another formidable resistance group was led by Marshal Tito. His fighters were called the Partisans. Unlike Mihailovic, Tito sought to organize Yugoslavs of all backgrounds to fight the occupiers.

The two groups tried to cooperate, but they couldn't. Unfortunately, while both groups were battling the Germans, Italians and Croats, they also fought each other.

Marshal Tito organized the resistance to Axis occupation during World War II. Here, he signs documents at his secret mountain retreat somewhere in Yugoslavia.

Both Mihailovic's and Tito's resistance groups attacked the Germans fiercely, and the Germans quickly replied with horrible brutality. In some places, Germans killed one hundred Yugoslavian civilians for every German soldier lost to the resistance. By the war's end, one out of every nine Yugoslavs had been killed.

Partisan Victory

Eventually, Tito's Partisans won the support of the United States, Great Britain, and the other Allies. Tito formed a council to set up a new Yugoslavian government when the war was over. With the aid of the Soviet Union, the Partisans overcame the Germans and established a new government with Tito at the head.

Tito promptly executed Mihailovic and stamped out all other opposition. Then he set up the government of Yugoslavia that existed until 1991 as the Socialist Federal Republic of Yugoslavia. It was a Communist state, with

President Tito: Post–World War II Leader

After the Axis defeat in World War II, Josip Broz (whose public name was Tito) became the leader of Yugoslavia's new government. As the nation's president for more than twenty-seven years, Tito was primarily responsible for balancing the different interests of Yugoslavia's many nationalities and holding the country together with a strong central government.

Born in 1892 in Kumrovec, Croatia (then part of Austria-Hungary), Tito was the son of two Roman Catholic peasants. His father was Croatian, and his mother was Slovene.

After his initial schooling was complete, Tito became a metalworker and then joined the local Social Democratic Party. In World War I, he was drafted into the Austro-Hungarian Army. After being wounded in combat, he was taken to a prison camp in Russia in 1915. Tito was still a prisoner when the Russian Revolution erupted in 1917, and he witnessed first-hand the violence and civil war that ensued.

In 1920, Tito returned to Croatia, where he first entered politics. By 1927, he had already been appointed secretary of the Zagreb central committee of the Communist party. As communism fell in and out of favour during the following years, Tito dodged those who saw him as a political threat. In 1934, he became a member of the Politburo—the Communist party's governing body—and acquired his code name of Tito.

Although Tito was gaining power during the late 1930s within the Communist party machine—both in Moscow and in Yugoslavia—his greatest political opportunity came with the outbreak of World War II. Defying the Axis powers, Tito organized a group of forces called the Partisans and mounted a highly successful Balkan resistance movement. The Partisans received aid from both the United States and Britain, and fought against German and Italian forces as well as the Yugoslavs, who wanted to return a king to the Yugoslavian throne.

By the end of World War II in 1945, Tito and his Partisans were in control of much of Yugoslavia. During that year, he became the premier and minister of national defence. Controlling both the Yugoslavian Communist party and the state's central government,

Tito was the most powerful individual in the country. In 1953, he was elected president. After serving as president for twenty-one years, he was elected president for life in 1974.

As the top official in the Yugoslavian government, Tito had some notable successes. Dedicated to an independent Yugoslavia, he managed to resist Soviet domination, even though he remained dedicated to communism throughout his life. He also managed to mediate a working peace between the many ethnic groups that populated Yugoslavia's various republics. Although longtime hatreds between Croats, Bosnian Muslims, Serbs, and Albanians always threatened Tito's coalition, the president was able to move a unified country forward for many years—sometimes only through the use of his strong persuasions.

When Tito died in May 1980, Yugoslavia's precarious coalition of ethnic groups became even more unsteady. For the decade that followed, a loosening of governmental control and a move toward "softer" communism enabled ethnic friction and conflict to intensify. In the early 1990s, those problems finally erupted into a full-scale and bloody civil war.

Hungary's president Janos Kadar joins Tito on a hunting trip in 1963.

the government in control of all business, agriculture, and most other aspects of life. The League of Communists was the only legal political party. Tito, in true hardline Communist fashion, would not tolerate ethnic and religious differences in the country. When Croats and Albanians agitated, he punished them harshly. Tito's goal was to create one nation, indivisible, at any cost.

As a Communist state, Yugoslavia had strong ties to the Soviet Union. But Tito had his own ideas about how his country should be run. In 1948, he split with the Soviets, and Yugoslavia became a nonaligned nation. Without the USSR as an ally, it was linked neither to the East nor the West. Tito, named president for life, developed a unique Yugoslavian form of communism.

As long as Tito lived, he held the country together by force. He balanced his government carefully between Eastern and Western powers. And he kept Yugoslavia's many rival groups in check. The country became so dependent on the iron hand of its president that, almost as soon as Tito died in 1980, Yugoslavia began to unravel.

The Republics Gain Power

After Tito, Yugoslavia was governed by a kind of "collective presidency". Each of the republics selected a representative to act as Yugoslavia's president in a rotating system. Each representative rotated as head of the Yugoslavian state for a year. Unless a president had Serbian support, however, he had very little power.

In the post-Tito era, the government "watered down" its communism. Some private enterprise was allowed, and the republics and their ethnic groups were given more power. The more power the republics got, the more they wanted. And republics such as Croatia and Slovenia began to resent the fact that the federal government was dominated by Serbs. Serbia, as it had been many times in the past, was the power in Yugoslavia.

Tito's death in 1980 created a great instability in the Yugoslavian government, which was headed by leaders from each of the republics on a rotating basis. Here, the flag of Yugoslavia covers Tito's coffin.

Rising Unrest

By the middle of the 1980s, anti-Serbian unrest was growing steadily in Slovenia, Croatia, and Kosovo. Islamic Albanians in Kosovo attacked Orthodox Serbs and their churches, and many Serbs were forced to leave. In Croatia and Bosnia, anger was also directed at Serbs. The federal government cracked down hard on civil protests, but unrest continued. At the same time, the country was beset by serious economic woes.

Inflation reached a staggering 80 per cent in 1984. Petrol had to be rationed and housing was scarce and very expensive. The cost of basic necessities rocketed, and luxuries, such as television sets, were almost completely out of reach for most people.

The desire of each republic to run its own affairs independently greatly disrupted the nation's industry and transportation. The railways, for example, were allegedly a national system. But the republics would not allow their own locomotives to be taken past their homeland boundaries. Each time a train crossed into another republic, the locomotive had to be changed.

The Socialist system created under the Communists was not working well. People were discontented. In 1984, for example, one western foreign journalist in Croatia and Slovenia found that even Communist officials complained about the government's handling of the economy.

Economic problems and unrest caused friction within the Communist party. Communists argued with fellow Communists, and political dissenters argued against everyone. Under the weight of great criticism and discontent, the Communist party collapsed, and many other parties were declared legal. In the short term, these circumstances may have been good for democracy, but they were not good for the Yugoslavian federation. Movements for greater independence in Slovenia and Croatia grew even stronger. The breakup of Yugoslavia was about to begin.

ODLUČIMO SAMI
O SUDBINI
SVOJE HRVATSKE

HDZ
Hrvatska demokratska zajednica

Chapter 3

The Breakup

Yugoslavia started to splinter in the late 1980s. In 1989, Franjo Tudjman was elected Croatia's president on a sovereignty platform, and in February 1991, Slovenia and Croatia declared that Yugoslavian law had no authority within their borders. Rapidly, the two changing republics moved toward autonomy.

As weeks passed, tensions approached boiling point. The federal government put its troops on combat alert and called up military reserves. Croatia and Slovenia began to mobilize their own military forces. The world looked on as Yugoslavia headed for the inevitable—war.

Military Forces

Before the war, the Yugoslavian army of the federal government numbered more than 169,000 soldiers, plus more than 500,000 reservists. In total, it was one of the largest armies in Europe. Most of the soldiers were young conscripts. The army, as well as the other armed forces, was dominated and led by Serbs.

Federal forces had immense firepower at their disposal. They had a large battery of modern warplanes—such as Soviet MIG fighters—tanks, and heavy artillery. Most Yugoslavian infantrymen carried the fully automatic AK-47 assault rifle.

> As soon as the unifying influence of Tito was gone, each republic began to reassert its individuality and independence.

Opposite:
Thousands of Croats rallied in support of Franjo Tudjman during the spring of 1989. Tudjman was soon elected president of Croatia with an overwhelming mandate to move his republic toward independence.

Much of the fighting against the Croats and Bosnians would be carried out by Serbian nationalist irregulars or militias. These were groups of armed civilians who mobilized under various leaders. Some were ordinary citizens. Several were former soldiers. Many of these groups were little more than gangs, some including criminals and citizens on the "fringes" of society. The leader of one group, the Serbian Volunteer Guard, was a Belgrade gangster.

The more formal military forces of the republics warring against the Serbs and the central government formed a large, diverse group. Some were reservists or federal army soldiers who sided with their own ethnic groups. Others were police from the republics. Many were militiamen. Irregulars and militias on both sides waged some of the most ruthless fighting. These were the forces that were accused of most of the war's most publicized atrocities.

Some irregulars acted as if they enjoyed playing soldier. They brandished their weapons for reporters, swaggered, and uttered boastful threats against their enemy. Their uniforms were often bizarre. One Serbian militiaman who beat Bosnian students in front of reporters wore a blue military uniform with a Beatles T-shirt.

Militias on all sides took on unique names. Many sounded like those of American street gangs. Among the better known groups were Black Legion, White Eagles, Serbian Tigers and the Green Berets (not related to the U.S. or British commandos). One Serbian militia fighting in Bosnia reached back to World War II for its name—Chetniks. The Chetniks were the resistance forces who opposed the Nazis and the Partisans of Tito.

The First Clashes

A Croat, Stipe Mesic, was scheduled to become head of the revolving presidency in late May 1991, but the Serbs blocked him. That action heightened already dangerous

Croat Stipe Mesic was scheduled to become president of Yugoslavia in May 1991 but was blocked by the Serbian-dominated government.

Slovenian soldiers in Ljubljana prepare for battle with the Serbs of the Yugoslavian federal army in June 1991.

tensions. Then Croatia and Slovenia declared their independence but did not actually secede from Yugoslavia. They said they would wait to see if a new federation of sovereign states could be arranged. Although talks and negotiations dragged on for the rest of the summer of 1991, the efforts failed.

Within days after the Slovenian and Croatian declarations, federal and Slovenian troops were clashing on that republic's borders. Meanwhile, units of the federal army that had been stationed in Slovenia were trapped there. This same situation would later develop in Croatia and Bosnia as well.

Other European nations soon began efforts to start truce talks, but they also began to side with the breakaway states. Germany and Austria, from the beginning, backed Slovenia and Croatia. Eventually, most Western nations and Russia were to do the same. These nations recognized the sovereignty of the new states and assigned them seats in the United Nations.

Some diplomats and political analysts suspect that the early support given to Slovenia and Croatia by European governments helped to actually trigger the war. These analysts say that Croatia thought the European Community would step in militarily to halt the Serbs. Believing this, the Croats fought on. At the same time, the Serbs also thought the EC would soon intervene, so they tried to grab as much land as they could before that occurred. The EC's intervention never happened, but the war did.

By late summer, Croatia's Mesic was allowed to assume the Yugoslavian presidency, but his was an office without power. By the autumn of 1991, the existing federal government had completely fallen apart. The Croatian and Slovenian presidents had walked out on the system, followed by the members of Parliament from the breakaway republics. At that point, the Serbians assumed control of what was left of the old Yugoslavian government.

Spurred by European nations, truce talks continued, on and off, throughout the war. Although the supposed goal was peace, the republics bickered endlessly, and trust was nonexistent. It seemed to many as if no one really wanted to avoid an all-out conflict.

When clashes between federal and Slovenian troops increased in the autumn of 1991, Portugal, the Netherlands, and Luxembourg mediated a truce. A short time later, federal troops withdrew unhindered from Slovenia.

Attempts to obtain a lasting truce between republics continued. In capitals around Europe, diplomats huddled in an effort to find a workable solution for Yugoslavia. But after more than a year of discussions, the world seemed no closer to peace in Yugoslavia. Without a solution, bloody war in the region seemed the only outcome.

Failed Talks

The federal government, and the Serbs, in particular, had little to gain by battling for Slovenia. Few Serbs live in the republic, which, as in the past, is closely tied to Austria. The federal government simply let Slovenia slip away.

Kosovo and Macedonia: Future Flashpoints?

The attention of the world focused primarily on fighting in Croatia and, then, in Bosnia. For some reason, the unrest in the Serbian province of Kosovo was all but ignored. Yet some observers believed that Kosovo could become the worst flashpoint for conflict in Yugoslavia. Although it was part of Serbia, Kosovo had considerable autonomy. Albanians started settling in Kosovo when the Serbs living there fled from the Turks in the seventeenth century. Today, Albanians outnumber Serbs nine to one. Most of Kosovo's ethnic Albanians are Muslims.

The Serbs in Kosovo claimed they were persecuted by the Albanian majority. Many Serbs have moved to other parts of Serbia. The Albanians contended that Serbia and its government had disregarded Albanian culture, religion and language.

In 1992 there was concern that if fighting occurred between Kosovo's Albanians and the Serbs, the conflict could ignite a far wider war. Albania could enter the war in support of its ethnic brothers and sisters. Some political groups in Kosovo favoured Bulgaria, making Bulgarian intervention another possibility. Others felt that Turkey, a Muslim country, might even move to protect the Muslims in Kosovo.

While tensions built in Kosovo, unrest began in the southernmost republic of Macedonia. Greece was not happy with Macedonian independence, which was declared in September 1991. Yugoslavian Macedonia borders a region of the same name in Greece. Because Greece and Turkey were never on good terms, it was feared that Kosovo and Macedonia would become yet another "Balkan tinderbox".

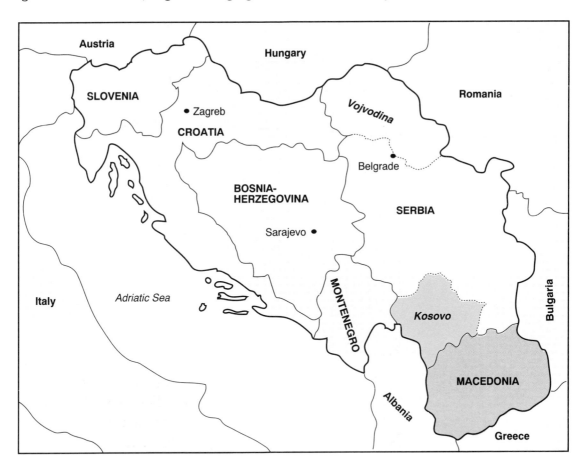

Croatia was another matter, however. There, the federal army backed up rebel Serbs in Croatia in an effort to hack out a piece of Croatia and make it a Serbian state. In the months that followed, the Serbians achieved this goal. A third of Croatia became the Republic of Krajina, a Serbian state. No other groups were tolerated in the new state. Neither Croatia nor other countries outside Yugoslavia officially recognized Krajina, but its existence was nonetheless a reality.

During the autumn of 1991, the European Community and the United States desperately tried to work out a compromise between the Serbian-dominated federal government and Croatia. But neither Serbia's president Milosevic nor Croatia's president Tudjman would budge. Meanwhile, the flames and destruction of war were slowly engulfing much of Croatia.

Charges of Brutality

Croat and Serb hatreds were inflamed by charges of atrocities on all sides. As the war continued, it became painfully clear that all parties were guilty. Serbs slaugh-

During the autumn of 1991, various world leaders attempted to mediate the conflict in Yugoslavia through diplomatic efforts. Serbian president Slobodan Milosevic (left) met with Russian president Boris Yeltsin (right) at the Kremlin in October of 1991.

tered innocent Croats and Bosnian Muslims. Bosnians and Croats, in turn, slaughtered many innocent Serbs. Each atrocity led to another, each for revenge and each fuelled by mounting hatreds.

A professor from the University of Zagreb in Croatia wrote to his colleagues in the West about tortured Croats "with pulled-out eyes, hearts taken out, cut limbs and sex organs," and called the Serbs "the dirtiest and most severe aggressor in the history of wars".

A Serbian professor accused the Croats of "genocidal behaviour". A Serbian literary critic also warned of the "genocide" of the Serbs, not just in Croatia, but also in Bosnia and Kosovo. "What is happening today is a barbarous attack on the vital existence of the Serbs," he wrote in a Belgrade newspaper.

Some Serbian newspapers raised the ugly spectre of neo-Nazism arising in Croatia and Slovenia. The Serbs had revived the term "Ustasha," the name of the pro-Nazi Croatian government in World War II, and attached it to the present government there. One writer even accused Germany of "financing, arming, and advising the Croatian neo-Nazi drive".

Early in the war, Serbian demonstrators had marched in Belgrade carrying placards against Croatia. Some carried signs with a drawing of Croatian president Tudjman. On his forehead was a Nazi swastika.

Ironically, as the war progressed, it was the actions of extremist Serbs that most closely mirrored what the Nazis had done to Jews during World War II. The extremist Serbs began a campaign of what they called "ethnic cleansing". They advocated the wholesale removal and slaughter of all Muslims and Croats from areas the Serbs wanted to control. Many Muslims and Croats were put into trucks and shipped away from their homes. Terrorized into leaving all that they held dear, they were then herded into prison camps. As part of this plan, Serbs settled in places that were cleared of Muslims and Croats.

Chapter 4

War in Croatia

It was a sunny September day in Montenegro. Sheep grazed on the green grass of the high hillsides. Trout flashed through the crystal waters of streams, some more than a thousand feet below the tops of the steep valleys they had cut into the earth. On the roofs of farmhouses, hams cured in chimney smoke. Above all this apparent tranquillity rose the limestone mountains of the region. These mountains had earned Montenegro its name, which means "black mountains".

Then through these black mountains came convoys of military trucks carrying young Montenegrin soldiers. They gripped their weapons, their faces as stony as the mountains through which they passed. They were on their way to a war that was being waged about eighty kilometres away, across the border on the Adriatic coast of Croatia.

The War Explodes in Croatia

Throughout the autumn of 1991, the war in Croatia burned ever hotter. The federal army and Croatian Serb rebels had been battling the Croats all summer. Fighting had been centred primarily in eastern Croatia, where most of the Croatian Serbs live. By September, however, the war had begun to spread. Federal troops, along with

Cities in eastern and southern Croatia suffered greatly in clashes with the Serbs.

Opposite:
Two young refugees from Dubrovnik, Croatia, cry aboard the ship that carried them away from their battered homeland. Dubrovnik, in southern Croatia, fell under heavy attack from the Serbian-dominated federal army.

mobilized Serbian and Montenegrin reservists, moved toward the palm-lined beaches and beautiful bays of the Adriatic. There, federal gunboats began to shell historic cities on the Adriatic coast of Croatia.

Some of the federal units cut across Bosnia. Tanks, armoured troop carriers, and mobile howitzers rolled down the mountain roads. Bosnian nationalist civilians set up roadblocks. Shots were exchanged, and Bosnian officials warned that Bosnia would fight back. As the conflict widened, the European Community continued to pressure Serbia's Milosevic and Croatia's Tudjman to make peace, but they would not. Cease-fires that had been arranged by the European nations quickly broke down. Croatian troops blockaded federal army barracks, cutting off food, water and electricity from the helpless units.

War in Eastern Croatia

During September, the hard-line Serbian generals who were running the federal army launched the biggest offensive the war had yet seen. In eastern Croatia, federal and Croatian Serb troops moved swiftly on three key cities—Vinkovic, Vukovar, and Osijek.

Soviet-made MIG fighter planes, tanks, artillery, and rocket launchers hammered away at Vinkovic, Vukovar, and Osijek. Entire neighbourhoods were reduced to rubble as the Croatians were heavily outgunned by the federal army. Occasionally, however, Croatian forces managed to capture federal tanks and heavy weapons. Nevertheless, one by one, major cities fell to the federal army and the Croatian Serbs.

By the end of 1991, the rebel Serb republic of Krajina was firmly in place in eastern Croatia. Croats fled or were forced out of the region, and Croatian cities like Vukovar "officially" became Serbian cities. The leaders of the new Krajina were so hard-line that even President Milosevic had problems with them.

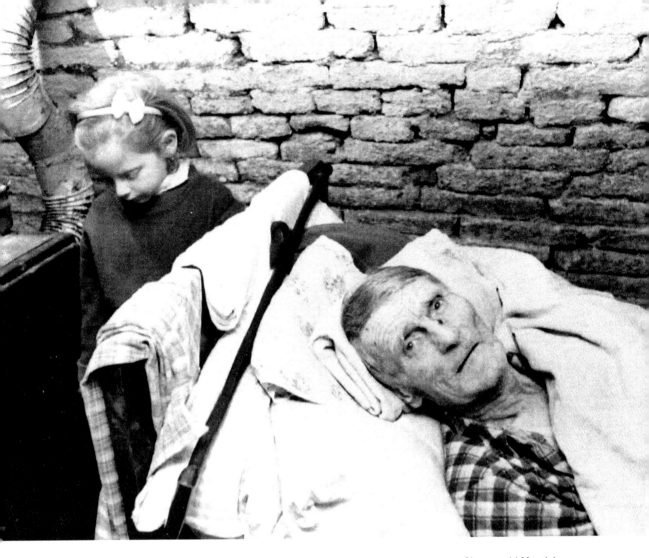

As eastern Croatia changed hands, the U.N. Security Council began work on a cease-fire that was finally accepted. A force of 14,000 U.N. peacekeepers moved into the region during the spring of 1992 to ensure the terms of the truce.

The U.N. force, from several countries, took control of four areas on the borders of territories that were held by Serbo-Croatian rebels. The peacekeepers managed to keep the warring sides apart and prevented the Serbs from extending their territory. Major fighting ceased, and the federal army pulled out. But the hatred remained despite the calm, and the problems that caused the bloodshed were still unresolved.

Six-year-old Magdalena Cutura stands beside her eighty-four-year-old grandfather in the cellar of their home in Osijek, Croatia. The family took refuge in their cellar while federal army troops shelled the town in December 1991.

The U.N. peacekeeping plan called for the Serbs in Krajina to eventually put down their guns. Croats who had fled would then be able to return to their homes. Meanwhile, an arrangement would be made to give the Serbs three guarantees against Croatian domination. Neither side liked the plan.

Objections were raised from both the Croatian and Serbian interests. The leaders of Krajina were intent on

During the spring of 1992, a large U.N. peacekeeping force moved into Croatia to police a cease-fire.

War on a Unique Environment

As Montenegrin reservists moved toward Dubrovnik, the Montenegrin parliament was meeting outdoors in the mountains of Durmitor National Park. The wilderness of the park is considered a "World Natural Heritage Site" by UNESCO, the United Nations Educational, Scientific, and Cultural Organization. The parliament was there to declare Montenegro an "Ecological State".

What on earth, you may ask, is an ecological state? According to the declaration, it legally places environmental concerns above "all our national, religious, political and other sentiments and convictions". Undeveloped and wildly beautiful, Montenegro promised its future development would be in harmony with nature. Montenegro's president, Miomir Bulatovic, recognized it was a strange time to declare peace with nature. But he added that "it is always the right time" to take steps to protect the environment.

Even as he spoke, however, federal units were pounding another UNESCO heritage site. Plitvice Lakes National Park in Croatia was battered and shut down. Near Osijek, yet another natural wonder was being destroyed. It was the Kopacki Rit Reserve, a vast wetland along the Danube. Kopacki Rit is a rest stop for hundreds of species of migratory birds. It was one of the finest birding areas of Europe.

Much of Yugoslavia, in fact, has great and varied natural beauty. Before the war, it was a favourite destination for European tourists. Within the country's 256,000 square kilometres are several different environments that range from palm-fringed beaches, on the Adriatic coast, to high mountains clothed in conifer forests.

The climate of the coast in southern Croatia and Montenegro is subtropical. Sheer limestone cliffs rise above the coast. Behind the cliffs are mountains, some more than 2,440 metres high, that are an extension of the Alps. Their climate is like that of central Europe. As the crow flies, the distance between palm trees and pine trees can be only twenty or so kilometres. The fact that the mountains rise so steeply from the coast accounts for the dramatic difference in climate.

Many other parts of Yugoslavia are also mountainous. Eastern Yugoslavia, however, is largely a flat plain, extending into Hungary.

Before the war, much of Yugoslavia was undisturbed wilderness.

Yugoslavia has vast wilderness areas, like Kopacki Rit and Plitvice Lakes. The country has wildlife that has vanished or become very rare in most of Europe. Bears and wolves still roam some areas. Wild boar and red deer are abundant. Rare griffon vultures still nest in certain mountain ranges. Lake Skadar, on the border of Montenegro and Albania, has hundreds of species of birds, including pelicans.

Yugoslavia has some of the cleanest rivers in Europe. They include some streams considered among the best in the world for trout fishing.

The war has taken its toll on nature. At Kopacki Rit, deer and other animals were machine-gunned. Trout were killed with dynamite at Plitvice. Explosive charges damaged fragile natural dams of limestone that separated the park's dozen or so lakes. Rare brown bears were shot down. Elsewhere forests were destroyed. The damage caused to the environment by the war—like the damage caused to the humans—will take much time to assess and even longer to heal.

A resident of Dubrovnik surveys the destruction of some of the city's oldest buildings—some of which dated to the Middle Ages. The damage was caused by shelling from the Yugoslavian federal army.

associating their state with Serbia, and the Serbs in Krajina supported this idea. Many Croats wanted the peacekeepers out. They urged their government to take Krajina. One Croatian political party that sought to renew the war wore the uniforms of Croatia's Nazi puppet state, fuelling Serb fears. The European Community attempted to set up negotiations between both sides, but by the end of the summer of 1992, little progress had been made.

War in Southern Croatia

Unfortunately, the U.N. cease-fire in eastern Croatia did not end the war in southern Croatia.

The centre of the fighting was the ancient walled city of Dubrovnik on the Adriatic. Dubrovnik is a strategic city, lying north of the beautiful Bay of Kotor, on the border with Montenegro. The Yugoslavian Navy is based in the bay.

The federal army moved against Dubrovnik at the same time as it hit the cities in eastern Croatia. From surrounding hills, artillery shells, mortar fire, and rockets rained down. Meanwhile, gunboats lobbed shells into the city from the sea.

The shelling of Dubrovnik provoked outrage among the nations of the world. Thousands of buildings and other structures—some of them over one thousand years old—were destroyed. All told, more than 4,000,000 artillery rounds were fired at the historic city and its suburbs. Because Croatian defenders resisted fiercely in Dubrovnik, shelling eventually dwindled. By the summer of 1992, however, shelling resumed. This time, Croatian forces took the offensive and drove the Serbians fifty kilometres back from the city. By the autumn, federal troops began to pull out of the region.

Although fighting in southern Croatia eventually wound down, Bosnia was still firmly engulfed in the war.

WHERE THE FIGHTING HAS BEEN

Chapter 5

War in Bosnia

In many ways, Bosnia was the most vulnerable republic in the war, and quite possibly the one with the most to lose. Some political analysts have suspected that, although they are enemies, Croatians and Serbians plotted to divide up Bosnia, which lies in between Croatia and Serbia. Indeed, as fighting progressed, Serbia took over two thirds of Bosnia, and Croats grabbed most of the rest. The new occupants proclaimed their regions to be semi-independent states. Some reports said that troops from Croatia were stationed in Bosnia but, overall, the Croatian takeover went almost unnoticed. This was so mainly because the world was horrified by the savagery of the Bosnian warfare with the Serbs.

A Bloody Spring

The most serious fighting in Bosnia began in the spring of 1992 after the Serbs tried to raise fears that Bosnian president Alija Izetbegovic was a Muslim extremist. They suggested that he wanted to revive the oppression of Serbs that had been suffered under the Turks.

Serbian rebels and federal army troops swarmed over the Bosnian countryside. They surrounded many major cities, including Sarajevo, site of the Bosnian government.

Caught between Serbia and Croatia, Bosnia was the most vulnerable republic in the war, and the one that suffered the most.

Opposite:
The bombed-out shell of an apartment building is a battered monument to the violence and destruction that overtook Sarajevo in Bosnia.

Hemmed in and full of refugees, the cities were subjected to a fearful siege. The territory held by Bosnian Muslims was reduced to a handful of cities and a few shreds of countryside. Rebel leader Radovan Karadzic, a psychiatrist and an extremist, declared that the Serbs would keep all land they conquered.

In May, the United Nations and the international community pressed Serbia's president Milosevic to withdraw federal troops, but the president did not comply. Instead, he ordered non-Bosnians among the troops to leave Bosnia. Some did, leaving their heavy equipment with the Serbian rebels. Moreover, 55,000 federal troops remained. They were allegedly Bosnian Serbs, but that could not be proved.

Serbian extremist Radovan Karadzic (centre) became a radical spokesman for the Serbian nationalistic cause. As the leader of Serbian forces fighting in Bosnia, Karadzic advocated the seizure of as much land as possible for a "Greater Serbia".

Bosnian President Alija Izetbegovic, a Muslim, was targeted as an enemy by the Serbs.

"Ethnic Cleansing" in Bosnia

As the war in Bosnia progressed, Serb extremists called for "ethnic cleansing". Areas claimed by Serbs were to be "cleansed" of Muslims and Croats. The non-Serbs were intimidated into leaving by threats of death and, often, by beatings and fiendish torture. Many were simply murdered. Many non-Serbs were forced to sign over all their property to the federal government. Entire villages were rounded up, put into stifling goods wagons, and shipped to Croatia. All told, more than a million Muslims were evicted from their homes in Bosnia. By the same token, Muslims and Croats expelled 300,000 Serbs from areas under Croatian or Bosnian control. Their methods were the same—force and cruel violence.

War Against Civilians

Because the ultimate goal of many extremists was ethnic cleansing, civilians were common targets. Seldom in modern times has a war been waged so fiercely against innocent, noncombatant civilians. In Sarajevo, for

Civilians of Sarajevo run for cover as fighting rages on in the streets. Noncombatant populations suffered greatly in all aspects of the war; thousands were killed, and tens of thousands were left wounded and homeless.

example, Serbian artillery repeatedly blasted civilian neighbourhoods that had no military significance. Serbian snipers shot civilian residents of the city as they walked on the streets. Citizens everywhere were murdered whether they were men, women or children; it made no difference. Even ambulances, supply trucks and other humanitarian vehicles came under fire.

Cut off by Serbs, people in Sarajevo suffered terribly. Food and medical supplies dwindled, and both water and electricity were cut off. Homes were turned to rubble.

The situation was equally bad in Gorazde, a Muslim city in southeastern Bosnia. Refugees nearly doubled its population of 40,000, even though the embattled city was surrounded and subject to constant bombardment.

Reports of Death Camps

As the war continued, rumours of Serbian-run death camps mounted. Fugitive Muslims told reporters about camps where thousands of their countrymen were imprisoned. The prisoners were said to be in squalid conditions, many reportedly left to suffer in their own filth. Reports also circulated that Serbian nationalists—the Chetniks— were systematically killing prisoners. Extermination was said to be by shooting, starvation, and beatings. Prisoners, reports said, were forced to beat one another and were subjected to many other humiliations.

World leaders expressed outrage at the death camp reports. Serbian leaders denied that such an extreme programme of extermination was under way, though they admitted that thousands of Muslims were being detained. They were quick to point out that, in turn, Muslims and Croats had imprisoned thousands of Serbs.

PRISON CAMPS IN BOSNIA

SLOVENIA

Zagreb CROATIA

Vojvodina

BOSNIA-HERZEGOVINA

Belgrade

SERBIA

Sarajevo

Adriatic Sea

MONTENEGRO

Kosovo

☐ U.N.-protected area
  Reported Serb-controlled camps
▲ Reported Muslim-controlled camps

U.N. Sanctions

In Belgrade, Milosevic asserted that he had no control over the Bosnian Serbs, but it was clear that they were receiving support and weapons from his Belgrade government. Meanwhile, the United Nations had voted economic sanctions against the newly reduced Yugoslavia made up of Serbia and Montenegro. No country could sell products or buy them from Yugoslavia. Most importantly, these sanctions meant that Yugoslavia could not import oil, which it badly needed. The sanctions also cut commercial airline links with Yugoslavia. Medical supplies were not included in the ban. These economic restrictions were to remain in place until Yugoslavia met all the U.N. demands, which included an end to interference in Bosnia and the disarming of all irregular forces there.

U.N. convoys carrying supplies fell victim to Serbian bombardments and sniper attacks during the war. Here, U.N. soldiers inspect the wreckage of vehicles that were destroyed during a peacekeeping mission.

Airlifts with Aid

Although the sanctions formally applied more international pressure to stop the war, they did not stop the fighting. By July 1992, however, international pressure enabled the United Nations to airlift food and medicine to Sarajevo. An arrangement allowed the Sarajevo airport to be taken over by 1,100 U.N. peacekeepers. Previously, the airport had been under Serbian control.

U.N. aircrafts began ferrying food and medical supplies to the Sarajevo airport, where they were convoyed into the city by U.N. soldiers. Meanwhile, the European Community continued to work for a cease-fire.

Food and medicine were collected and distributed by the United Nations and the International Red Cross throughout much of the war. Most of the aid was flown into the Sarajevo airport and was distributed to desperate regions in Bosnia.

Mercy missions were repeatedly interrupted by aggression and local militias who soon established check points where they would search aid convoys and collect 'taxes'. This would often mean long negotiation and sometimes convoys would have to turn back. The disaster which began to unfold was seen on television screens worldwide and at once there was a huge public response. Soon, there were many private trucks and ambulances delivering aid but in October 1992, as conditions became more and more dangerous, the first U.N. troops were sent to protect the aid convoys. At first, convoys were attacked and blocked mostly by the Serbs but in 1993, as the conflict between the Bosnian Croats and Muslims began to flare up, check points were erected by all sides.

The Intervention Question

The first approval for use of air power to protect aid convoys was voted on at the United Nations in August 1992. How to stop the war became an increasingly thorny question for the international community. NATO voted to send up to 11,00 troops, if necessary, to protect relief efforts, but there was a hollow ring to these proclamations. Warships from Europe and the United States were sent to the Adriatic, but as vessels were only there to 'observe' whether or not the U.N. sanctions were obeyed, again it was an empty gesture. By the end of 1992 there were over 8,000 U.N. troops in Bosnia with a limited authority and only lightly armed. In this way, the troops soon became hostages, which made the Western governments reluctant to approve any policies which could endanger these vulnerable soldiers.

The United Nations Expels Yugoslavia

By the autumn of 1992, the republics of Serbia and Montenegro were all that remained of Yugoslavia. Because the country had changed beyond all recognition and

Opposite:
Captured civilians await instructions during a U.N.-supervised prisoner exchange in Sarajevo.

President Slobodan Milosevic: Puppetmaster of Conflict

Many political analysts considered Serbia's president Slobodan Milosevic the grand orchestrator of the nation's bloody civil war. Known to many as a ruthless and power-hungry leader, Milosevic had fanned flames of hatred created by long-standing ethnic divisions and had rallied the nationalistic feelings of his Serbian compatriots. He had also stirred Serbian nationalists to take whatever action was necessary to promote the Serbian cause of unification—both ethnically and geographically. His ultimate goal was to unite all the Serbs of the region into one new country that would include not only the republic of Serbia, but also territory that had been carved out of the other neighboring republics. Many who knew him testified that Milosevic would attain any goal—and at any cost. A European diplomat, quoted in a *Time* magazine article, said of Milosevic, "Nothing interests him but Serbian success, even if it means tens of thousands of dead and dispossessed."

Throughout his political career, Milosevic had built a reputation for knowing where the power lies and how to seize it. His more than thirty years in Yugoslavian politics showed him to be a master of persuasion and power brokering.

Born in a small town near Belgrade in 1941, Milosevic was the unhappy child of a father who was a religious teacher and a mother who was a fervent Communist. Early in his childhood, his father abandoned the family by moving to Montenegro, where, a few years later, he committed suicide. Soon after his father's death, Milosevic lost an uncle to suicide as well. When his mother took her own life in 1974, Milosevic nearly had a complete emotional and physical breakdown.

Before the 1970s, however, Milosevic had already firmly established himself in Yugoslavia's elite Communist inner circle. His political star began to rise when he befriended Ivan Stambolic, the nephew of one of Serbia's most powerful Communist leaders. For nearly twenty years, Milosevic ascended the party hierarchy, in large part due to the good graces of Stambolic. Eventually, Milosevic was made Belgrade

chief of the Communist party, and then boss of the Serbian Communist party. By 1989, he was the unchallenged president of Serbia, which, due to ultimate Serbian control of the federal government, meant Milosevic was the practical head of Yugoslavia.

For many of his years in public office, Milosevic worked hard to solidify Serbian national pride. In 1987, he was sent to the Serbian province of Kosovo, where local Serbs complained of mistreatment by the Albanian majority. As angry Serbs fought with police, Milosevic dramatically appeared on a balcony and addressed the crowd. "No one has the right to beat people!" Milosevic insisted. Then, in a show of courage, he descended into the crowd and repeated his message over and over again. That day, many political analysts have said, was a turning point in Milosevic's career. "From that day the balance changed," wrote Slavolijub Djukic, a biographer of Milosevic. "He knew how to touch the Serb's national feelings." In less than a year, Djukic added, "he moved from being a second-rate politician to almost a god."

Perhaps more than any single person, Milosevic was responsible for the savage bloodshed and destruction that characterized the civil war in his country. As the consummate double-talker, Milosevic insisted that his intentions were to keep Yugoslavia together rather than to tear it apart. But his actions betrayed a much different objective. On one hand, he insisted that he was not trying to create a Greater Serbia, yet much evidence pointed to the fact that it was Milosevic's order that sent aggressive Serbian forces into Croatia and later to Bosnia. While Milosevic was publicly swearing that no Serbian people were involved in Croatian and Bosnian violence, a local newspaper published photographs of a Belgrade guerrilla force in the war-ravaged Bosnian city of Bijelinja.

Although public opinion throughout the world seemed to be strongly against him, Milosevic remained undeterred in his objective. In an attempt to deflect criticism, Milosevic was fond of painting the Serbs as threatened and mistreated by non-Serbian peoples. Because the Serbs have dominated the

Yugoslavian federal government as well as the overall population, few found Milosevic's pleas remotely convincing. As he paid lip service to peace, Serbian forces in Bosnia and Croatia continued to hammer away at Croatia and Bosnia, inflicting large-scale murder and torture each and every day. Just how many people were going to die before Milosevic felt he had attained his goals was uncertain. What was certain, however, was that Serbia's president would

not concede his fight for Serbian self-rule and domination easily. As one official from the U.S. State Department was quoted in *Time* as saying, "For him, the word *compromise* is a dirty word, meaning treason and surrender." The terrible reality of that sentiment was that, for thousands of Slavs on all sides of the conflict, compromise would have only meant a welcome end to unspeakable tragedy and human suffering.

Serbian president Slobodan Milosevic.

because the ruling government was the obvious aggressor in the widening war, on 22 September 1992 the U.N. General Assembly voted 127-6 in favour of withdrawing membership of the Serbian-dominated Yugoslavia. The expulsion of Yugoslavia was meant to send a strong message to Milosevic's government. There was a growing number of reports of atrocities that took place in Serbian-held territories, particularly those carried out in the prison camps at Omarska, Manjaca and Trnopolje which aroused strong public protests in the West. Although the U.N. and Western governments wanted to believe that the expulsion would motivate the Serbian leadership to work for peace, many people close to the Yugoslav presidency feared that this gesture would do very little.

Towards the end of 1992, the West was split on the question over the enforcement of the U.N. - imposed "no-fly-zone", which had time and again been defied by the Serb aircraft repeatedly bombing and strafing Muslim towns and villages. A hawkish Germany and U.S. lined up against those urging caution at further international military involvement – an unusual combination including France, Britain and China. Russia, ominously (in the light of history), issued a warning that she would "not stand by and see Serbia crushed".

The Negotiations

In late October 1992 the European community and UN negotiators, Lord Owen and Cyrus Vance, produced the first detailed proposal for political settlement. The idea was that there would be a set of self-governing "cantons", with the central government responsible only for national defence and foreign affairs. The merits of this plan were that refugees should be able to return to their homes and that the "Serbian" cantons would not connect in such a way to make it easy to join them together into a Greater Serbia. But reality was that already these proposed cantons were joined together and Serbian military leaders would never sacrifice these links.

Division of Bosnia

Bosnian Serbs were strongly encouraged by the Milosevic government to sign the Vance-Owen plan at the special meeting in Athens on 12 May 1993 because the plan was seen as a step towards full integration with Serbia. One Serbian politician commented "It is just the first stage. It is not going to last too long. Not even Lord Owen believes it". But opposition among the Bosnian Serb politicians and military leaders, particularly General Mladic, was too strong and in a referendum of 15 May the plan was rejected.

On 22 May the final death warrant to Bosnia was signed in Washington when the Vance-Owen plan was

Two schoolchildren walk down a street in Vukovar, Croatia, devastated during the war.

abandoned and it was decided that the remaining two million or so Bosnian Muslims would be allowed to gather in the so-called "safe areas", where they would be guarded by the U.N. troops. But these troops were only allowed to return fire if they were shot at, not if Muslims needed protection. President Izetbegovic commented that the international community had proclaimed a new code of behaviour in which force is the first and the last argument.

Over the summer months Presidents Milosevic and Tudjman and Lord Owen put forward a series of cruder plans for division of Bosnia into three statelets. Each version contained a scattered territory left for the Muslims but this kind of settlement was not acceptable to the uprooted and determined Muslim soldiery. Even Lord Owen described such an arrangement as "not an ideal solution".

Operation Irma and the Plight of Refugees

In August 1993, the siege of Sarajevo continued much in the same way as in the months before, water and electricity were only very rarely available and daily life for most people was concentrated on obtaining the basic necessities. Life was especially hard for children: schools had stopped working a year before and many children did not know what had become of their families and friends. Summer months were hot and there was nowhere safe to play. Serbs regularly bombarded the city from their positions in the surrounding hills and in one such incident a little girl called Irma was seriously injured and her mother was killed outright.

With serious spinal and head injuries, Irma had no chance of survival if she stayed in the primitive conditions of Sarajevo hospital. It was the end of July and the beginning of what is known as the silly season for the news industry. On a Sunday evening in August, a news report of Irma's plight on BBC television had a dramatic effect. As calls began to pour into Downing Street, Prime Minister John Major ordered an RAF Hercules to bring Irma, her father and sister to Britain. On Monday evening Irma was in London's Great Ormond Street children's hospital undergoing an operation. The prime minister's intervention was followed by other countries and since then some 2000 beds have been offered in more than 20 countries. Ms Sylvana Foa of the United Nations High Commisioner for Refugees said that the change in attitudes after 16 months of indifference from western countries was like "day following night".

At the same time, in August 1993, the International Court of Justice in the Hague was considering Bosnian accusations that Serbs had been carrying out a campaign of territorial expansions through ethnic cleansing and genocide. Four months previously, a similar accusation by the Bosnians resulted in a court order to stop the genocide. Although the court does not have any powers to enforce its orders, traditionally its decisions carry diplomatic and moral weight. Meanwhile, at the U.N., the work on collection of evidence to bring about prosecution for war crimes committed in Croatia and Bosnia hardly progressed, hampered by lack of resources and, some said, the political will.

International Politics Fail

As peace talks broke down yet again in August 1993, Lord Owen, the EC mediator, blamed the threat of NATO air strikes for the stalled talks. The reasoning was clear: the proposed peace was no longer based on any principle other than recognition of each party's military strength, therefore anything that leads either party to believe that it may improve its position militarily will only delay the conclusion. Pressure was applied on the Bosnian Government to accept the principle of ethnic partition and by September the Muslim community agreed, while at the same time rejecting the partition map and insisting that Muslim territories seized by force should be returned. It was unclear, however, whether President Izetbegovic would sign the peace plan or hold out for more land concessions.

Nato Warns of Air Strikes

Clashes on the ground in Bosnia continued and the siege of Sarajevo carried on with its own grim momentum of bombardment and deprivation. By October the U.S. Secretary of State, Mr Warren Christopher, again warned the Serbian President Milosevic of possible NATO air strikes if the Serbs continued to strangle Sarajevo. In New York meanwhile, the U.N. Secretary General Dr. Boutros Ghali met the new U.N. mediator, Thorvals Stoltenberg, to discuss the options in case the peace plan failed. This pessimism was echoed at the seat of negotiations, Geneva, where, struggling to inject new momentum, the mediators were now conducting talks behind closed doors.

Serbia's Power Play

Mr. Milosevic meanwhile appeared convinced that a peace agreement would formalize his "victory" and hasten the lifting of the U.N. sanctions against Serbia. These sanctions, imposed 17 months earlier and coupled with two years of war, had devastated Serbia's economy. In October 1993, the inflation rate was calculated at 1,896 per cent per month, which meant that the annual rate of inflation was somewhere around 20 million per cent, the worst in the world since the Second World War.

In an effort to present a more acceptable image to the world, in July President Milosevic had appointed a Serbian-born naturalized American citizen, Milan Panic, as the prime minister of rump Yugoslavia. By September 1992 nobody was in doubt that Mr Panic had good intentions and but that his stay as the prime minister would be limited. In December 1992 presidential elections were held and Mr Milosevic duly claimed victory, although international observers were concerned at indications of abuse of the electoral system.

In December 1993 other elections were held, this time they were parliamentary elections, with a much less clear-cut outcome. Despite claiming a triumph, President Milosevic's party failed to win an outright majority and together the opposition parties emerged stronger.

Since the start of the Bosnian peace talks in 1992, international mediators have counted on President Milosevic to keep his Bosnian Serb protégés in control who, by continuing to refuse to give Muslims enough land for a viable state, ensured that they were not overlooked in any peace settlement.

Lieutenant-General Rose Arrives at Sarajevo

As winter of 1994 took hold on Bosnia, conditions steadily worsened. The Belgian general commanding the U.N. forces in Bosnia announced that he wished to leave his post earlier than scheduled. It was time to grasp the nettle and get tough. Lieutenant-General Sir Michael Rose was the man, a Falklands hero toughened through active service with the SAS in the Middle East. His first moves were a brilliant success, a column of armoured Warriors forced open the Serb-controlled route into Sarajevo while NATO jets stood by in case of an attack. But one Saturday morning in January, a mortar bomb came sailing out of the sky and into the Sarajevo market. Sixty-four people died in an instant. Although as many died regularly from shellling each week, this was enough for NATO. It ordered the Serbs to pull back their heavy guns or face air strikes. U.S. President Clinton promised to send its air force jets to strengthen NATO's forces. The guns were drawn and it was a case of who would blink first. And then, the unexpected happened. Almost

Smoke rising from a building under attack in Gorazde in April 1994

forgotten and ignored in the international decision-making on Bosnia, Russia announced on 17 February that it was to despatch its peace-keeping troops to Sarajevo under the U.N. flag in exchange for withdrawal of Serbian artillery. With Russian soldiers taking their place, Serbian forces withdrew. Helping Serbs to obey the U.N. ultimatum was an important decision which also signalled that the old East-West differences were not dead and buried. Moscow had made it clear that no decision can be reached in Bosnia without its agreement.

But also, by forming a buffer zone around Sarajevo, at a stroke Lieutenant-General Rose transformed his troops from mere convoy escorts into peace-keepers.

Almost immediately after, there was an even greater success, when in Washington Presidents Tudjman and Iszetbegovic signed an agreement which ended the war between Croats and Muslims. A first step towards an alliance between Bosnia and Croatia, this agreement buried the Owen-Stoltenberg plan (formerly referred to as the Owen-Vance plan) and confirmed the loyalty of the great majority of the Bosnian Croats to Sarajevo. It showed too the Bosnians' determination to resist the aggressors at home as well as the map-makers in Geneva. Lieutenant-General Rose's men were spread out on the Croat-Muslim front lines and the delicate cease-fire was maintained.

But soon came the Serb attack on Gorazde and the mirror cracked. In May 1993, the U.N. had proclaimed Gorazde one of the six "safe areas" but when the Serb attack came in April 1994 the U.N. at first did nothing and the world gnashed its teeth. Then, belatedly, the U.N. asked NATO for the right to call air strikes to defend all five "safe areas" but Moscow strongly opposed the move. As Serbs ignored all international pleas and continued to bombard helpless civilians of Gorazde from a safe distance, NATO planes, guided to their targets by a small company of British soldiers, bombarded Serb artillery targets. Many people applauded but others accused Lieutenant-General Rose of causing a serious break in American-Russian relations. The political masters at the U.N. were not pleased and the Serbs were clearly upset.

The Conflict Goes On

In spite of a warning by Russia's President Yeltsin, Serbs continued to bombard Gorazde. In retaliation for air strikes, Serbs also decided to hold some 200 U.N. personnel as hostages. As the attack advanced, the town of Gorazde, now without water, electricity or even the basic medicines, was enduring what can only be described as a humanitarian tragedy.

Eventually the Bosnian Serb forces retreated, which removed the need for NATO air strikes but the U.N. refused to say whether all the heavy guns had been pulled out of the exclusion zone.

By summer, fighting in Bosnia erupted regularly while the international community continued to bicker. A 'Contact Group' was formed and by the end of July it proposed a new peace plan. The plan was accepted by the Bosnian and the Croatian Governments, and endorsed by President Milosevic, only to be rejected by the Bosnian Serb leader Radovan Karadjic. The pattern of events established during the siege of Gorazde began yet again to repeat itself. Fighting erupted in central Bosnia where Bosnian Government forces made some gains. In retaliation, Serbs from Bosnia and Croatia attacked the U.N.-protected area of Bihac, which was mercilessly bombarded from a safe distance while its citizens starved. NATO wanted to respond using air strikes but the U.N. opposed this. This time the Western world was shaken by the severity of the U.N.-NATO dispute over the chain of command in Bosnia. The U.N. won the argument on the day, thus eliminating any further possibility of military intervention, or an imminent lifting of the arms embargo, but larger questions over the role of NATO and the U.N. remained unresolved.

With 300,000 dead (including 70,000 children) and over two million displaced persons, and material destruction that can only by calculated in billions, it is important to keep in mind that the resolution of the war in Bosnia is not only a matter of practical negotiations over percentage of territory. Preoccupied with disagreements within its international institutions, the West wished that the Bosnian issue would be settled through some practical territorial division, but such a pragmatic approach fails to take account of the need to uphold the fundamental principles of international law and order. As many Bosnians would say, if peace is to be workable there also has to be justice.

Chronology

Fifth Century	Tribes of Slavs move to the Yugoslavian region from the Carpathian Mountains.
Seventh-Ninth Centuries	Slavs are dominated by foreign peoples, paving the way for religious differences.
Late 1300s	Ottoman Turks invade regions that were later to become Serbia, Bosnia, Montenegro and Macedonia.
1878	Serbia gains independence.
1912	Serbia, Bulgaria, Montenegro, and Greece drive the last of the Turks out of Yugoslavia.
1914-1918	Serbia fights Austria-Hungary, Germany, and Bulgaria during World War I. After the war, a new country, called the Kingdom of Serbs, Croats, and Slovenes, is formed and headed by King Alexander.
1929	King Alexander declares himself dictator of a new country to be called the Kingdom of Yugoslavia. He is assassinated in 1934.
1939	Croatian unrest leads to Croatia self-rule.
April 10, 1941	Coatia proclaims itself an independent state.
1941	The Kingdom of Yugoslavia is invaded by the Axis forces.
1941-45	While resistance fights the forces of fascism, there is also a civil war going on. Fascist forces withdraw completely by 1945.
1945	Socialist Federal Republic of Yugoslavia is formed. Tito, leader of the victorious partisans, is its leader.
1948	Tito splits with the Soviet Union, and Yugoslavia becomes non-aligned.
May 1980	Tito dies, lessening the Communist hold on Yugoslavia.
1984	Economic problems and unrest cause the collapse of Yugoslavia's Communist party.
June 1991	Croatia and Slovenia hold referenda and decide that they will seek independence from the Yugoslavian Federation.
Summer 1991	Clashes continue in Slovenia and Croatia. Many towns are bombarded by the Yugoslavian National Army's heavy artillery, especially the Adriatic resort of Dubrovnik, and in eastern Croatia, the town of Vukovar. Serbs commence campaign of "ethnic cleansing". A cease-fire is negotiated though the U.N. in the Krajina, central and eastern Slovenia.
January 15, 1992	The European Community formally recognizes the sovereign republics of Slovenia and Croatia.
Spring 1992	After a referendum, Bosnia proclaims independence and is recognized by the international community and the U.N.. Immediately afterwards, the Serbian community begins to fight the elected government of Bosnia-Herzegovina. The siege of Sarajevo begins.

July 1992	Rumours of Serb death camps are confirmed by British journalists. The United Nations begins airlifts of food and aid to Sarajevo. Milan Panic becomes prime minister of Yugoslavia but is unable to make constructive changes.
September 1992	The U.N. General Assembly withdraws membership for Serbian-dominated Yugoslavia.
October 1992	NATO provides troops to help U.N. forces in Bosnia.
November 1992	No-fly zone is imposed.
Spring 1993	War develops between the Bosnian Croats and Muslims.
May 1993	Bosnian Serbs reject the Vance-Owen Plan.
August 1993	Operation Irma takes place. Peace talks break down.
December 1993	Elections held in Serbia. President Milosevic's party does not retain overall majority.
January 1994	Lieutenant-General Sir Michael Rose arrives in Sarajevo. A shell kills 64 people in Sarajevo market.
February 1994	NATO issues ultimatum to the besieging Serbs to withdraw from Sarajevo or face air strikes. Russians intervene and Serbs withdraw heavy artillery from the hills surrounding Sarajevo.
April 1994	Serbs attack Gorazde which is one of the U.N. proclaimed "safe areas".
May 1994	The United States, France, Germany, Britain and Russia form a "contact group".
July/August 1994	Contact Group proposes division of territory which is rejected by Bosnian Serbs.
November 1994	Bosnian Government forces make gains in central Bosnia but Serbs besiege the U.N.-protected area of Bihac. NATO carries out limited air strikes but is opposed by the U.N.. The siege continues.
December 1994	Bangladeshi U.N. soldier in the Bihac pocket is killed by Serb artillery. Civilians continue to suffer and new Serb prison camps are discovered. NATO decided to reinforce its military forces on the ground and there will be no pull-out in the foreseeable future.

For Further Reading

Noel Malcolm, *Bosnia: A Short History,* Macmillan, 1994.

Mark Thompson, *A Paper House: the Ending of Yugoslavia,* Vintage, 1992.

Ed Vulliamy, *Seasons in Hell: Understanding Bosnia's War,* Simon & Schuster, 1994.

Christopher Cviic, *Remaking the Balkans,* The Royal Institute of International Affairs, Pinter Publishers, 1991.

Index

Acknowledgements and photo credits

Cover: Wide World Photos; pp4, 10: © Andrew Reid/Gamma-Liaison: p. 12: © Nigel Chandler/Gamma-Liaison; p 15: Giraudon/Art Resource; pp. 16, 17 (left), 20, 21, 24, 32, 35: AP/Wide World Photos; pp17 (right), 18: Culver Pictures, Inc.; pp. 22, 26, 27, 30, 38, 46, 51: Wide World Photos; p.36: © Richards/Gamma-Liaison; p. 37: © Kathleen Campbell/Liaison International; pp. 40, 43: © Lee Malis/Gamma-Liaison; p. 42: © Hodson-Spooner/Gamma-Liaison; p. 44: © Keith Bernstein/Gamma-Liaison; pp. 47, 49: Noel Quida/Gamma-Liaison; pp53, 58 Associated Press/Topham; Maps by Sandra Burr.